Welcome 

Let's celebrate our cherished companions! The connection between humans and their beloved pets, especially dogs, has blossomed over the years. Nowadays, countless individuals regard their dogs as integral family members, nurturing a profound and loving relationship with them. Consequently, the health and happiness of our loyal four-legged friends have taken center stage in our lives. A vital aspect of ensuring our dogs thrive is offering them a proper and balanced diet.

Throughout the ages, the realm of canine nutrition has experienced a remarkable evolution. While dry food, in the form of kibble or pellets, stands as a favored and practical choice, it has become increasingly clear that a fresh, natural diet can offer a wealth of health advantages for our beloved companions. Just as humans would not find satisfaction in consuming only one type of dry food throughout their lives, dogs too thrive on a diverse array of nutrients and flavors.

Natural dog food embodies the philosophy of offering fresh, wholesome ingredients, including premium proteins and nutrient-dense vegetables, to fulfill their nutritional requirements in a more satisfying and flavorful manner. Picture a human being confined to a diet of only oats for their entire life; it would be dull and devoid of the vital nutrients necessary for optimal health. The same principle applies to our canine companions; by diversifying their meals with fresh components, we grant them the gift of a more fulfilling and health-enhancing culinary journey.

In the modern landscape, numerous pet food companies prioritize profit over the quality of the ingredients they incorporate into their offerings. This focus can result in a diminished variety and quality in the diets of our beloved dogs. Yet, within our own kitchens and refrigerators, we often find an abundance of fresh, nutritious ingredients that are perfect for canine health. The high-quality proteins we enjoy, including chicken, turkey, salmon, and lean beef, hold immense benefits for our furry companions. Similarly, vegetables brimming with vitamins and minerals, such as carrots, peas, spinach, and sweet potatoes, can serve as wonderful enhancements to their meals.

The concept of crafting fresh meals for our dogs transcends mere nutrition; it embodies a profound expression of love and devotion. By dedicating our time and energy to create wholesome food for our furry companions, we demonstrate our commitment to their happiness and health. Offering our dogs fresh ingredients not only enhances their lives but also deepens the connection we share with them, reinforcing the beautiful bond that unites us.

Dog nutrition plays a vital role in the lives of our beloved companions, and it is essential to reflect on the quality and diversity of the meals we offer them. A wholesome, fresh diet, rich in high-quality proteins and nourishing vegetables, can be a brilliant choice to promote the well-being and joy of our furry friends. By embracing a more tailored approach to our dogs' nutrition, we can guarantee they enjoy the balanced and delightful meals they truly deserve.

If you've ever found yourself questioning which foods are suitable for our beloved canine companions, you are in the perfect spot. Here, I share with you a collection of 25 simple recipes, crafted especially for dogs aged 2 years and older. Remember, portion sizes may differ based on your pet's breed and weight, so keep the following details in mind:

Proteins:

Small breeds: It is advised that approximately 20-30% of the daily caloric intake for small breed dogs should be derived from protein. This can fluctuate based on age and activity level. Puppies and young dogs might need a bit more protein.

Large breeds: For dogs of larger stature, a slightly reduced percentage is typically advised, hovering around 18-25% of total caloric intake as protein. Once more, individual requirements may differ.

Carbohydrates:

Small Breeds: For small breed dogs, carbohydrates can constitute around 30-60% of their daily caloric intake, influenced by their activity level. These carbohydrates serve as a vital source of energy, fueling their playful spirits and vibrant lives.

Large Breeds: For our majestic large breed dogs, carbohydrates can typically fall within a range of 30-60% of their daily caloric intake. Their needs may fluctuate depending on their activity levels and various other factors.

These recipes not only present a delightful array of flavors and nutrients, but they also empower you to play a vital role in your beloved companion's well-being. Together, we can guarantee that our furry friends savor fresh, delectable meals that will enhance their joy and health for many years ahead.

Chicken accompanied by
vibrant vegetables

Recipe 1

Ingredients:
200 grams of skinless chicken breast
100 grams of carrots, diced into delightful morsels
100 grams of vibrant peas
Reduced Sodium Chicken Broth

In a medium saucepan, bring a suitable amount of water to a rolling boil. Gently place the 200 grams of boneless chicken breast into the saucepan. For an enhanced flavor, feel free to add some skin and cartilage. Allow the chicken to cook thoroughly. Once done, carefully remove the chicken from the saucepan and set it aside. In the same flavorful water, introduce the 100 grams of carrots, chopped into small pieces, along with the 100 grams of peas.

Sauté the vegetables for approximately 10 minutes, or until they reach a tender perfection. Carefully lift the vegetables from the water and allow them to cool for a few moments. To elevate the flavor of this delightful dish, incorporate a splash of low-sodium chicken broth to taste. At last, present this exquisite blend of chicken breast, carrots, and peas in a warm embrace of chicken broth.

Turkey delights in a savory sphere.

Recipe 2

Ingredients:
200 grams of finely ground turkey
1/2 cup of wholesome oats
100 grams of vibrant spinach
1 egg

In a spacious bowl, blend together 200 grams of ground turkey, 1/2 cup of oats, 100 grams of finely chopped spinach, and 1 egg. Use your hands to mix all the ingredients thoroughly, ensuring they are completely combined. From this mixture, shape small meatballs to your preferred size. Preheat the oven to the suggested temperature. Arrange the meatballs on a baking sheet that has been greased or lined with parchment paper.

Bake the meatballs until they reach a perfect golden brown and are fully cooked, typically taking around 10-15 minutes based on their size. Once they are ready, take the meatballs out of the oven and allow them to cool for a few moments before serving. These turkey meatballs infused with oats and spinach present a wholesome and delightful choice for your beloved pet. Relish the joy as your dog savors this delightful treat!

Salmon paired with roasted
sweet potato

Recipe 3

Ingredients:
200-250 grams of salmon fillet, a delightful choice for a nourishing meal.
Medium-sized potato
100 grams of vibrant broccoli

Preheat your oven to the ideal temperature. On a baking tray, arrange the salmon fillet, half a sweet potato, and 100 grams of broccoli. Bake these delightful ingredients until they are perfectly cooked, which typically takes around 20 to 25 minutes, depending on the size and strength of your oven. While the ingredients are baking, you can simmer the sweet potatoes in a pot until they become tender and can be transformed into a smooth puree.
Once the salmon, sweet potatoes, and broccoli have been cooked to perfection, allow them to cool for a few moments.

Blend the cooked sweet potatoes until they transform into a velvety, uniform puree. Present the salmon fillet next to the creamy sweet potato mash and vibrant, cooked broccoli.

Beef and vibrant spinach

Recipe
4

Ingredients:
200 grams of tender, lean beef
100 grams of Spinach
100 grams of vibrant carrots
1 Pure yogurt, unsweetened

In a spacious saucepan, bring 200 grams of lean beef to a boil in water until it reaches perfect tenderness. Afterward, let the beef cool down. Once it has cooled, chop it into small, delightful pieces. In a bowl, combine the cooked beef with finely chopped spinach and carrots, also diced into small morsels.

Incorporate the plain, unsweetened yogurt into the blend. Yogurt contributes a velvety, creamy consistency while enhancing the nutritional benefits.
Present this delightful snack to your dog, ensuring it is at a safe temperature for enjoyment.

Tender Chicken and
Velvety Sweet Potato

Recipe

5

Ingredients:
Half a chicken breast
100 grams of delightful sweet potatoes
100 grams of zucchini, a vibrant green treasure of nature.

Steam the half chicken breast until it reaches perfect doneness, ensuring that the juiciness and nutrients are beautifully preserved. As the chicken steams, bring the sweet potatoes and zucchini to a gentle boil until they become tender, which typically takes around 20 minutes. Once the chicken, sweet potatoes, and zucchini are ready, allow them to cool for a few moments. Slice the cooked chicken breast into delightful bite-sized pieces. Present the chicken breast pieces alongside the tender sweet potatoes and zucchini on a plate, creating a vibrant and nourishing meal.

This delightful recipe for steamed chicken breast paired with sweet potatoes and zucchini offers a wholesome and balanced choice for your beloved pet. Ensure the food is at a safe temperature for enjoyment, and witness the joy as they savor this lovingly crafted meal just for them.

Savory meatloaf accompanied
by vibrant carrots

Recipe 6

Ingredients:
200 grams of tender, lean ground beef
1 egg
1 shredded carrot
100 grams of oats, a nourishing foundation for your day.

Preheat the oven to the suggested temperature. In a spacious bowl, blend together 200 grams of lean ground beef with 1 beaten egg, the grated carrot, and 100 grams of oats. Stir all the ingredients until they are thoroughly mixed.

Gently pour the mixture into a well-suited baking tin, crafting it into a delightful cake shape. Place the cake in the preheated oven and let it bake until it reaches perfection, typically taking 25-30 minutes. Remember, baking time can fluctuate based on the size and strength of your oven, so ensure the cake is completely cooked through. Once it has reached that golden moment, take it out of the oven and allow it to cool for a few moments before sharing its deliciousness.

Turkey and sweet potatoes
roasted to perfection in the oven

Recipe 7

Ingredients:
200 grams of finely ground turkey
A portion of sweet potato
1 crimson pepper

Prepare 200 grams of boneless ground turkey using one of the following methods: you can bake, boil, or air fry it. Ensure the meat is thoroughly cooked before moving forward. If you choose the air fryer, cook half a sweet potato at 375 degrees Fahrenheit for 10 minutes until it reaches tenderness. Should you not have an air fryer, baking or boiling the sweet potato until it is fully cooked is a great alternative. Roast or steam a red bell pepper until it becomes tender. Allow all the ingredients to cool for a few moments. Dice the turkey meat into bite-sized pieces. In a bowl, blend the turkey meat pieces with the cooked sweet potato and red bell pepper. Serve this delightful mixture in a temperature-safe manner for your beloved pet.

Steamed fish accompanied by tender zucchini

Recipe 8

Ingredients:
1 pristine white fish fillet (boneless)
100 grams of wholesome brown rice
A portion of zucchini

In a frying pan, sear the white fish fillet of your choice, ensuring it is boneless and cooked to perfection. You may opt for pink fish or any white fish that calls to you. Prepare 100 grams of brown rice by following the instructions on the packet, typically involving boiling the rice in water until it reaches a tender state. As the rice simmers, chop half a zucchini into small, delightful pieces. Once the fish and rice are ready, and the zucchini is chopped, allow them to cool for a few moments. Gently flake the fish fillet into small, inviting pieces.

Blend the flaked fish, brown rice, and zucchini in a bowl. Present this delightful blend in a temperature-safe way for your beloved pet.

Hearty chicken and vibrant vegetable soup

Recipe 9

Ingredients:
Two succulent chicken thighs
Two vibrant carrots
1/2 cup of vibrant green peas
half squash
Reduced Sodium Chicken Broth

In a saucepan, gently simmer the chicken thighs alongside vibrant carrots, sweet peas, and fresh zucchini in low-sodium chicken broth. This broth will infuse the soup with a delightful and nourishing essence. Allow the mixture to cook over medium heat until the vegetables are tender and the chicken is perfectly cooked. Once the cooking is complete, carefully remove the bones from the chicken thighs, ensuring that the soup is free of any remnants.

Allow the soup to cool for a few moments before presenting it to your beloved pet.

Chicken and rice patties

Recipe 10

Ingredients:
200 grams of tender, shredded chicken breast
100 grams of cooked brown rice, ready to nourish.
100 grams of finely chopped spinach
1 egg (optional, to unite the mixture)

In a bowl, combine 200 grams of shredded chicken breast. Incorporate 100 grams of previously cooked brown rice into the bowl. Fold in 100 grams of chopped spinach to the mixture. For an extra touch, consider adding an egg to help bind the ingredients, making it simpler to shape the burger.

Combine all ingredients using your hands until they harmonize beautifully. Form the mixture into a patty of your preferred size.

Allow the burger to rest for a few moments before presenting it to your beloved pet.

Chicken and pumpkin delights

Recipe 11

Ingredients:
100 grams of cooked chicken breast
100 grams of cooked pumpkin
2 tablespoons of oats
1 egg

Preheat your oven to the ideal temperature. In a bowl, combine 100 grams of cooked chicken breast, 100 grams of cooked pumpkin, 2 tablespoons of oats, and 1 egg. Ensure that all the ingredients are thoroughly blended. From the mixture, shape small meatballs to your preferred size and arrange them on a baking sheet that has been greased or lined with parchment paper.

Place the meatballs in the preheated oven, allowing them to transform into a fully cooked and golden brown delight, typically taking around 20-25 minutes, depending on their size. Once they have reached perfection, take them out of the oven and let them cool for a few moments before presenting them to your beloved pet.

Savory beef and sweet potato broth

Recipe 12

Ingredients:
200 grams of tender, lean beef
A portion of sweet potato
A portion of zucchini
2 cups of savory low-sodium beef broth

In a spacious saucepan, bring together 200 grams of lean beef, half a sweet potato, half a zucchini, and 2 cups of low-sodium beef broth. This broth will infuse the soup with rich flavor and essential nutrients. Allow the mixture to simmer over medium heat until the beef is thoroughly cooked and the vegetables are delightfully tender.

Ensure the beef is thoroughly cooked and safe for consumption.

Savory Turkey and Spinach Delight

Recipe 13

Ingredients:
200 grams of ground turkey, lean and free from bones or excess fat.
50 grams of vibrant spinach
100 grams of perfectly cooked quinoa

Steam 200 grams of ground turkey until it reaches full doneness, ensuring that there are no bones or excess fat present in the meat. As the turkey steams, prepare 100 grams of quinoa by following the package instructions, which typically include boiling the quinoa in water until it becomes tender and fully cooked.

Steam the 50 grams of spinach until it reaches a tender state. After the turkey meat, quinoa, and spinach have been cooked, allow them to cool for a few moments. Serve this delightful mixture in a temperature-safe manner for your beloved pet.

Oven-roasted fish and vibrant
pumpkin

Recipe 14

Ingredients:
1 fillet of boneless white fish (such as hake or pink fish)
100 grams of pumpkin
100 grams of vibrant broccoli

Preheat the oven to the ideal temperature. On a baking tray, arrange the boneless white fish fillet. Surround the fish fillet with 100 grams of pumpkin and 100 grams of broccoli on the same tray.

Place the ingredients in the preheated oven and allow them to transform until the fish is perfectly cooked and the vegetables are tender and golden, a process that typically takes around 20-25 minutes.

Once cooked, take the ingredients out of the oven and allow them to cool for a few moments.

Present this delightful medley of fish, squash, and broccoli to your pet in a way that ensures it remains at a safe temperature.

Savor the delightful combination
of grilled beef and sweet potatoes.

Recipe 15

1 tender beef fillet
100 grams of delightful sweet potatoes
100 grams of perfectly cooked green beans

Preheat your grill to the ideal temperature. Lay the lean beef steak upon the grill and allow it to cook until it reaches perfection. Ensure that the meat is thoroughly cooked for safety.

As the steak sizzles and transforms, take the opportunity to prepare the sweet potatoes in your preferred style, whether it be grilling or another method, until they reach that perfect tenderness. Similarly, let the green beans bask in your chosen cooking technique until they too become delightfully tender.

Once the beef steak, sweet potatoes, and green beans are perfectly cooked, allow them to cool for a few moments. Present this delightful medley of lean beef, sweet potatoes, and green beans in a temperature-safe manner for your beloved pet.

Salmon with a vibrant pea puree

Recipe 16

Ingredients:
200 grams of salmon fillet, a delightful treasure from the sea.
100 grams of vibrant peas
100 grams of cooked brown rice, ready to nourish.

Prepare the 200 grams of salmon fillet until it reaches perfect doneness. Whether you choose to bake, grill, or cook it in your preferred style, the choice is yours.

Prepare 100 grams of peas alongside 100 grams of previously cooked brown rice. After cooking, allow the ingredients to cool for a few moments. Flake the cooked salmon fillet. In a spacious bowl, combine the flaked salmon, peas, and cooked brown rice. Blend everything together until you achieve a smooth, uniform puree.

Serve this puree with care, ensuring it is at the perfect temperature for your beloved pet.

Sautéed veal accompanied by
mushrooms

Recipe 17

Ingredients:
200 grams of tender beef, diced into cubes
100 grams of mushrooms
Peppers (optional, according to your preference)
Half a cup of cooked brown rice, ready to nourish.

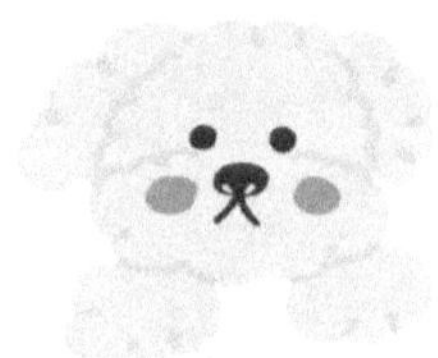

Heat a spacious frying pan over medium heat. Introduce the 200 grams of diced beef to the pan and sauté until it reaches perfect doneness. Ensure that the meat is thoroughly cooked for safety.

As the meat sizzles and transforms, take this moment to introduce the mushrooms and peppers, if you choose, allowing them to sauté until they reach a tender perfection. Gently fold in the 1/2 cup of previously cooked brown rice, blending all the elements harmoniously. Let it simmer for a few more minutes, inviting the flavors to unite in a delightful embrace.

Allow the mixture to cool for a few moments before presenting it to your beloved pet.

Turkey and
broccoli delight

Recipe 18

Ingredients:
200 grams of finely ground turkey meat
100 grams of vibrant broccoli
Pumpkin
2 cups of wholesome turkey broth with low sodium

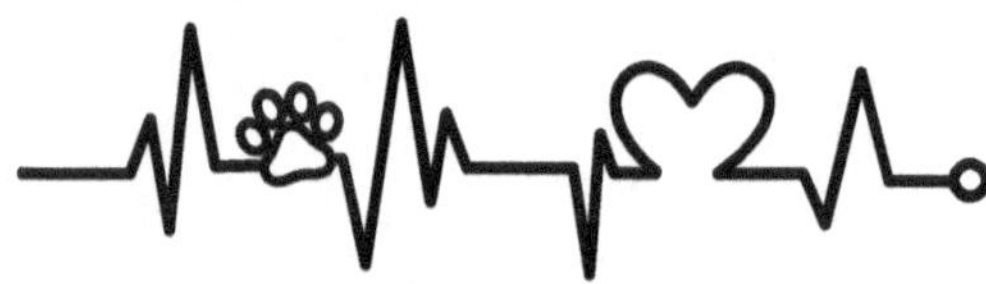

In a spacious saucepan, blend together 200 grams of ground turkey, 100 grams of broccoli, diced squash, and 2 cups of low-sodium turkey broth. The broth will infuse the soup with a delightful flavor.

Sauté the mixture over medium heat until the turkey is perfectly cooked and the vegetables are delightfully tender.

Ensure that turkey meat is cooked to perfection and safety. Allow the soup to cool for a few moments before presenting it to your beloved pet.

Garden-fresh chicken
and vibrant vegetable
medley salad

Recipe 19

Ingredients:
200 grams of tender, shredded chicken, perfectly cooked to perfection.
A small bunch of spinach
Half a grated carrot
A half apple, chopped into pieces
Plain natural yogurt (optional, as a topping)

Prepare and shred 200 grams of chicken, ensuring it is thoroughly cooked and safe for consumption.

In a spacious bowl, blend the shredded chicken with a generous handful of fresh spinach, half a grated carrot, and half of the diced apple.

If you desire, you can adorn the salad with a touch of plain, unsweetened yogurt as a dressing. This will infuse it with an extra burst of flavor. Blend all the ingredients together until they harmonize beautifully. Present this delightful salad to your beloved pet.

Savory Turkey with Vibrant Green Beans

Recipe 20

Ingredients:
200 grams of finely ground turkey
100 grams of vibrant, steamed green beans
1 cup of cooked brown rice

In a pan, add the 200 grams of turkey meat and cook it until it reaches perfection. Ensure that the turkey is thoroughly cooked for safety. While the turkey is sizzling, take the opportunity to prepare the 100 grams of vibrant steamed green beans.

Prepare 1 cup of brown rice following the instructions on the package.
When the turkey, green beans, and rice are perfectly prepared, combine all the ingredients in a spacious bowl.

Allow the mixture to cool for a few moments before presenting it to your beloved pet.

Salmon paired with creamy mashed sweet potatoes

Recipe 21

Ingredients:
1 salmon fillet
a delightful sweet potato
Half a zucchini, finely diced
Half a cup of low-salt fish broth

In a medium pot, gently prepare the salmon fillet and sweet potatoes until they reach a tender perfection. You may choose to boil them or employ any method that delights your culinary spirit. As they cook, take the opportunity to chop half a zucchini into small, vibrant pieces.

Once the salmon and sweet potatoes are perfectly cooked, transfer them to a large bowl and incorporate the chopped zucchini. Pour in half a cup of low-sodium fish broth. Blend all the ingredients together until you achieve a velvety smooth puree. Let the puree cool for a few moments before delighting your pet with this wholesome treat.

Chicken and ricotta cheese

Recipe 22

Ingredients:
A portion of cooked and shredded chicken breast.
2 tablespoons of creamy low-fat cottage cheese
A small bunch of spinach

Sauté half a chicken breast, cut into small pieces, until it reaches perfect doneness. Ensure that the chicken is cooked to safety.

In a bowl, combine the tender, shredded chicken breast with 2 tablespoons of low-fat cottage cheese.

Toss a handful of spinach into the bowl and blend all the ingredients together until they harmonize beautifully.

Present this delightful and nutritious meal to your beloved pet.

Fish accompanied by a velvety
pumpkin puree

Recipe 23

Ingredients:
1 pristine white fish fillet, free of bones
1 cup of tender, chopped pumpkin
Once-prepared peas
Low-sodium fish broth (for flavor)

Prepare the white fish fillet, ideally boneless, until it reaches perfect doneness. You have the freedom to bake, broil, or use any method that delights you. Cook 1 cup of squash until it becomes tender, then chop it into pieces. Prepare the peas following the instructions until they are tender.

In a spacious bowl, combine the cooked fish, diced pumpkin, and tender peas.

Incorporate a touch of low-sodium fish stock to enhance the flavor of the puree, then blend it until it reaches a velvety smoothness.

Savory lamb meatballs served alongside wholesome brown rice

Recipe 24

Ingredients:
100 grams of cooked brown rice, ready to nourish.
A small bunch of spinach
1 egg

In a spacious bowl, combine 200 grams of lean ground lamb, 100 grams of cooked brown rice, a handful of fresh spinach, and one egg.

Blend all ingredients until thoroughly unified. Shape the mixture into small meatballs.

Arrange the meatballs on a baking sheet and roast them until they are perfectly cooked through.

Allow the meatballs to rest for a few moments before presenting them to your beloved pet.

Turkey with a vibrant fruit medley

Recipe 25

Ingredients:
200 grams of tender, shredded turkey meat, perfectly cooked
Half a cup of chopped pineapple
Half a cup of sliced strawberries
A small bunch of spinach

In a spacious bowl, combine 200 grams of cooked and shredded turkey meat with half a cup of diced pineapple, half a cup of sliced strawberries, and a handful of fresh spinach. Blend all the ingredients until they are harmoniously united. Present this delightful salad to your beloved pet.

This delightful homemade turkey salad, featuring pineapple, strawberries, and spinach, is a wholesome and tasty choice that will surely bring joy to your dog. Ensure the salad is at a safe temperature for serving, and witness the happiness as your furry friend savors this lovingly crafted meal made just for them.

Moreover, these extra recipes provide you with even more opportunities to diversify your dog's diet with fresh, wholesome ingredients.

Chuches

Carrot and Apple Delights:

Ingredients: Vibrant carrots, crisp apples.

Grate the vibrant carrots and crisp apples, blend them together, and shape into delightful balls. Chill in the refrigerator before presenting.

Oatmeal and Banana Delights:

Ingredients: Wholesome oats, perfectly ripe bananas.

Combine oats and banana, shape into cookies, and bake until golden and crisp.

3. Enchanted Pumpkin Cubes:

Ingredients: Gourd of the season.
Cut the pumpkin into delightful cubes and steam or bake them until they reach a tender perfection.

4. Chicken and Broccoli Delights:

Ingredients: Tender chicken, vibrant broccoli.
Combine shredded chicken and broccoli, shape into balls, and chill in the refrigerator.

5. Delightful Sweet Potato and Oatmeal Cookies:

Ingredients: Potatoes, oats.
Cook and mash sweet potatoes, blend with oats, shape into cookies, and bake to perfection.

6. Crisp Apple and Vibrant Carrot Sticks:

Ingredients: Crisp apples, vibrant carrots.
Cut apples and carrots into delightful sticks and serve them fresh.

7. Turkey and Zucchini Delight:

Ingredients: Roasted turkey, zucchini.
Directions: Combine shredded turkey with diced cooked zucchini, and serve with joy.

8. Salmon and Spinach Delights:

Ingredients: Flaky salmon, vibrant spinach.
Roll fresh spinach around succulent pieces of cooked salmon, then slice into delightful rolls.

9. Savory Chicken and Brown Rice Delights:

Ingredients: Tender chicken, wholesome brown rice.
Combine shredded chicken with brown rice, shape into balls, and place in the refrigerator.

10. Turkey and Pea Medley:

Ingredients: Savory turkey, vibrant peas.
Cut the turkey into delightful pieces and blend them with tender, cooked peas.

HAPPY
BIRTHDAY

Canine Celebration Cake with Ground Meat

Ingredients:

1 cup of savory cooked ground meat (chicken, beef, or lamb are excellent selections)
1/4 cup finely shredded carrot
1 egg
1/4 cup of rolled oats, a wholesome foundation for your day.
1 tablespoon of liquid gold
1/4 cup of unsweetened applesauce (for frosting) Dog biscuit bone (for decoration, optional) Directions:

Begin by preheating your oven to a warm 180°C (350°F) and lovingly grease a small dish that is safe for both the oven and microwave.

In a bowl, blend the cooked minced meat, grated carrot, egg, rolled oats, and olive oil. Ensure that all the ingredients are harmoniously united.

Gently pour the mixture into the mold, ensuring it is spread evenly for a perfect finish.

Place your creation in the preheated oven and allow it to bake for about 20-25 minutes, or until a toothpick inserted into the center emerges clean. If you choose to use the microwave, set it to medium power and cook for 4-5 minutes.

Allow the cake to cool entirely.

Once the cake has cooled, generously spread the unsweetened applesauce over the top, resembling a delightful frosting. If you desire, you can adorn it with a charming dog biscuit bone.

Present your dog with his unique food bowl and cherish this special day together!

Vegan Celebration Cake for Dogs

Ingredients:

1 cup of velvety, cooked and mashed sweet potato
1/4 cup finely shredded apple
1/4 cup finely shredded carrot
1/4 cup of oat flour
1/4 cup of whole wheat flour
1 tablespoon of liquid gold coconut oil
1 teaspoon of peanut butter (free from xylitol)
1 teaspoon of rising magic
1/2 cup pure applesauce (for frosting)

Instructions:

Begin by preheating your oven to a warm 180°C (350°F) and lovingly grease a small dish that is safe for both the oven and microwave.

In a spacious bowl, combine the cooked and mashed sweet potato, grated apple, grated carrot, oat flour, whole wheat flour, melted coconut oil, peanut butter, and baking powder. Ensure that all ingredients are blended harmoniously.

Gently pour the mixture into the mold, ensuring it is spread evenly for a perfect finish.

Place your creation in the preheated oven and allow it to bake for about 20-25 minutes, or until a toothpick inserted into the center emerges clean. If you choose to use the microwave, set it to medium power and cook for 4-5 minutes.

Allow the cake to cool entirely.

Once the cake has cooled, generously spread the unsweetened applesauce over the top, creating a delightful layer reminiscent of frosting.

Present your dog with his unique food bowl and cherish this special day together!

This delightful vegan birthday cake for dogs offers a wholesome and tasty way to commemorate special moments without the use of animal-derived ingredients. Ensure that the ingredients are safe for your furry friend, and don't hesitate to consult your veterinarian if you have any questions about your pet's dietary needs.

Tips

Consult your veterinarian: Prior to altering your dog's diet or incorporating new foods, it is essential to engage with your veterinarian to guarantee that you are offering a balanced and secure diet for your beloved companion.

Diversity of ingredients: Much like us, dogs thrive on a diverse diet. Embrace a colorful array of fresh ingredients, including lean meats, vibrant vegetables, succulent fruits, and wholesome grains.

Proper proportions: Ensure that you offer the right balance of protein, carbohydrates, and fat in your dog's diet. These proportions will differ based on your pet's age, size, and activity level.

Proper cooking: Prepare ingredients with care to prevent any contamination. Ensure meat reaches the appropriate temperature and that vegetables are cooked thoroughly to support digestion.

Steer clear of specific foods: Certain foods can be harmful to dogs, including chocolate, grapes, onions, and garlic. It's essential to be aware of which foods to keep away from them.

Perfectly sized: Chop the ingredients into small morsels, making them easy for your dog to enjoy and digest, particularly if he is a puppy or has delicate teeth.

Hygiene: Rinse all ingredients meticulously before you begin your preparation. Maintain a pristine kitchen to prevent any cross-contamination.

Allergens: Be mindful of potential food allergies in your dog and make adjustments as needed. Introduce new ingredients one at a time to monitor for any possible allergic reactions.

Supplements: Based on your dog's dietary needs, it may be essential to incorporate vitamin supplements to guarantee he receives all the vital nutrients.

Watch your dog: Keep a close eye on your dog after altering his diet to ensure he is adjusting positively and displaying no signs of discomfort.

Nourishing Delights for Dogs

Lean meat: Lean meats serve as a remarkable source of high-quality protein. This vital nutrient is crucial for the formation and repair of tissues, the growth of muscles, and the maintenance of overall health. Additionally, it supplies essential amino acids that play a pivotal role in cellular function.

Vegetables: Carrots, spinach, and broccoli are vibrant sources of vitamins such as A and C, along with essential minerals and antioxidants. These nourishing elements play a crucial role in supporting a dog's immune system, promoting eye health, aiding digestion, and ensuring a radiant skin.

Fruits: Fruits such as apples, bananas, and blueberries offer a delightful array of nourishing nutrients, including essential vitamins and powerful antioxidants. They also serve as a wonderful source of fiber, vital for maintaining digestive wellness.

Eggs: Eggs serve as a comprehensive source of protein, delivering all the essential amino acids that our canine companions require. They are also abundant in healthy fatty acids and vital nutrients such as choline, which plays a crucial role in supporting brain health.

Oats: Oats serve as a remarkable source of slow-release carbohydrates. They offer dogs a steady supply of energy and are gentle on the digestive system. Additionally, they can be beneficial for dogs facing digestive challenges.

Coconut oil: Coconut oil is rich in beneficial fatty acids, including lauric acid, which can enhance the vitality of your dog's skin and coat. Additionally, it has been linked to remarkable anti-inflammatory and antibacterial qualities.

Yogurt: Sugar-free, lactose-free yogurt serves as a treasure trove of beneficial probiotics that nurture intestinal health in dogs. Additionally, it provides a rich source of calcium and protein.

Pumpkin: Pumpkin is a treasure trove of fiber, offering remarkable support for dogs' digestion. It serves as a gentle remedy for issues like constipation or diarrhea, harmonizing the rhythm of intestinal transit.

Fish oil: Fish oil is a treasure trove of omega-3 fatty acids, including eicosapentaenoic acid (EPA) and docosahexaenoic acid (DHA). These remarkable fatty acids promote vibrant skin, a lustrous coat, and robust joint health, while also offering powerful anti-inflammatory benefits.

Liver: In modest portions, liver serves as a remarkable source of iron and B vitamins, including vitamin B12. These vital nutrients play a crucial role in the production of red blood cells and the functioning of our cells.

Common human foods that pose risks or dangers to dogs

Chocolate: Holds theobromine and caffeine, substances that are harmful to dogs and may lead to heart and neurological issues.

Grapes and raisins: Even in small quantities, they can lead to kidney failure in dogs.

Onions and garlic: These foods harbor compounds that can harm red blood cells and lead to anemia in dogs.

Avocado: Persin, a compound present in avocados, has the potential to be harmful to dogs and may lead to gastrointestinal issues.

Xylitol: A synthetic sweetener present in numerous sugar-free products, including chewing gum and baked goods. It has the potential to trigger excessive insulin release, resulting in hypoglycemia in dogs.

Macadamia nuts: These pose a significant danger to dogs, potentially leading to weakness, vomiting, and tremors.

Coffee: The caffeine found in coffee poses a significant risk to dogs, potentially leading to serious heart and neurological issues.

Alcohol: The consumption of alcohol can lead to severe consequences for dogs, such as poisoning and liver damage.

Cooked Bones: Cooked bones have the potential to splinter, leading to blockages, harm to the gastrointestinal tract, or severe injury to a dog's mouth and throat.

High-salt food: An overabundance of salt can lead to salt poisoning in dogs, posing significant risks to their well-being.

Junk Food: Rich and salty treats, like chips or fast food, can lead to digestive issues and pancreatitis in our beloved dogs.

Dairy Products: A significant number of dogs are unable to properly digest lactose, leading to discomfort and digestive issues.

Hard-boiled eggshells: Hard-boiled eggshells can break into tiny, sharp fragments that may harm a dog's gastrointestinal system.

Green Onions: Often referred to as scallions, these delightful greens harbor thiosulfate, a substance that poses a risk to our canine companions.

Moldy Foods: Foods that have developed mold can harbor mycotoxins, which pose a risk to our beloved dogs.

Corollary

As a proud parent of four delightful dogs, I have always prioritized the well-being of my beloved pets, viewing them not merely as companions but as cherished members of my family. Throughout the years, I have encountered challenges stemming from a lack of knowledge and proper guidance in caring for my loyal friends. My unwavering goal has been to ensure they lead joyful lives and to extend the precious time we share together. I have come to realize that the love, commitment, and time devoted to my dogs are invaluable, resulting not only in fewer trips to the vet—bringing financial relief to our family—but also in their happiness and overall well-being.

These recipes are crafted not just for our beloved dogs, but for the enjoyment of the entire family. This signifies that we are engaging in an endeavor that uplifts every member of the household, with the sole distinction being the amount of salt used in the preparation. In today's world, many families may perceive a fresh diet for their pets as an added expense, yet it is essential to recognize that unique protein sources, like chicken gizzards and liver, are readily available in any supermarket. Furthermore, it is not a requirement to cook for your pets every single day. Personally, I prepare meals for the whole family 2-3 times a week. I express my gratitude to God for the wonderful family I have been blessed with and for the chance to share these recipes that nourish all the cherished ones in my home.

This book has been crafted in accordance with the meticulous steps and guidelines set forth by the Spanish Veterinary College Organisation (OCV). The OCV passionately advocates for a balanced and comprehensive diet for companion animals, acknowledging that proper nutrition is essential to the health and happiness of our beloved pets.

Bobby y Bear
DEDICATED TO
Drew
Willi